The Expository Writing Handbook

The WIN Program

The acronym *WIN*, the phrase *Writing in Narrative* and all titles in the *WIN - Writing in Narrative* series are copyrighted. No part of any book in the series may be duplicated by any means with the exception of the template pages. These pages are meant to be filled in by the student and may be duplicated if additional pages are needed for the *exclusive* use of the purchasing family.

The Expository Writing Handbook
By Dr. Leslie Simonson
First edition ©1996
©1998 ISBN 1-884098-14-2

The Elijah Company

1053 Eldridge Loop
Crossville, TN 38558
Phone 888/2-ELIJAH
Fax 931/456-6384
E-mail elijahco@elijahco.com

Types of Writing Covered in the WIN Program

Narrative Writing

Narrative Writing is also known as "Creative Writing" and is usually referred to as a "story." This type of writing may be either fiction or non-fiction and is commonly introduced as soon as the child can commit thoughts to paper. Three levels of the WIN Program cover Narrative Writing:

The Dictation Book introduces story writing to non-writers by having them dictate to a teacher or parent.

The Seven Sentence Story teaches story-writing fundamentals to beginning writers by guiding them through the steps of writing a story with only seven sentences.

WIN Level II is for upper elementaries and up. It teaches more advanced story writing techniques, based on the model of the Seven Sentence Story.

Expository Writing

There are two types of expository writing: the *research paper* and the *non-research paper*. The *research paper* is usually assigned at the middle school through high school level and begins with a topic to investigate, a problem to solve, or a question to answer. A short research paper is referred to as a "report," while a longer paper involving more extensive research over a greater period of time is commonly called a "term paper." The conclusions shared in this type of writing are based on factual material gathered by the writer through a variety of resources, and the author must list and credit his or her sources of information. The author is expected to follow specific guidelines in the presentation of the paper, even to the smallest details of margin size, footnote placement, and so forth.

The second type of expository writing involves little or no research. There are two forms of non-research expository writing: the *expository composition* and the *essay*.

An *expository composition* explains, describes, or provides information on a topic. It tells what something is, what it is like, and/or how it works. A computer software manual, instructions on how to train a dog (or accomplish some task), an attempt to interpret a portion of Scripture, or an informative piece about a selected topic (such as a book report)—these are all examples of an expository composition.

An *essay* may also explain, describe, or provide information on a topic, but it does so in the context of presenting the author's opinions and personal experience concerning the topic. The most common essay form begins with a problem to solve or a question to answer (for example: "Are home schoolers properly socialized?") and then presents the writer's opinions concerning solutions to the problem or answers to the question.

A report (such as a book report, news article, interview, etc.) may either be a research paper, an essay, or an expository composition, or may contain elements of all three, depending on how much research was involved and on whether or not the report expresses the author's opinions.

Two levels of the WIN Program cover expository writing for middle school ages and older: *The Expository Composition Handbook* and *The Essay Handbook.*

THE EXPOSITORY WRITING HANDBOOK

How to Write an Expository Composition

By
Les Simonson, Ed. D.

Edited by Pat Langley and Ellyn Davis

TABLE OF CONTENTS

INTRODUCTION

What is Expository Writing?

Expository writing is writing which explains something. In the subject of English, the term "composition" means a written work. Thus, an "expository composition" is a written work which explains something–what it is, or how it works, and so forth. Such compositions may cover a wide range of topics–people, places, animals, events, sports, weather, history, or whatever the author wants to write about. Because an expository composition is based on fact, the writer may want to do some background reading about the chosen topic.

An expository composition **is**:
- Writing based on fact
- Writing that explains something
- Writing that is expressed in the author's own words
- A composition that is approximately 500 to 600 words in length
- A composition with three main parts: an Introduction, a Main Body, and a Closing

An expository composition **is not**:
- A research paper, and has no footnotes or bibliography
- Writing based on the writer's personal opinion

How is an Expository Composition Arranged?

An expository composition has three parts: an **Introduction**, a **Main Body**, and a **Closing**. The Introduction is usually only one paragraph, the Main Body usually contains from two to six paragraphs, and the Closing is usually one paragraph. The composition should be approximately 500 to 600 words long. The different parts are arranged as follows:

Title:

I. **Introductory Paragraph** - tells about...
   A. Composition Topic
   B. Supporting Fact(s)/Detail(s)
   C. Purpose of Composition

II. **Main Body** - contains 2 - 6 Paragraphs. Each paragraph tells about...
   A. Composition Sub-Topic
   B. Supporting Fact(s)/Detail(s)
   C. Summarizing Statement that either
   –(First Choice) Draws a logical conclusion from the information presented in the paragraph **or**
   –(Second Choice) Restates the first sentence in the paragraph using different words

III. **Closing** - tells about...
   A. Restates the Purpose of the Composition using different words
   B. New Idea suggested or implied by the composition
   C. Significant Conclusion from information presented in the composition

What are the Steps in Expository Writing?

Pre-Step 1:   **Select a Topic**
                     Decide on Sub-topics
                     List each Sub-topic on a separate page. Number each Sub-Topic.
                     Jot down ideas and information about each Sub-topic
                     Adapt the ideas and information to Step 1

See page viii, FIRST, SECOND, THIRD, and FOURTH, for an explanation of the Pre-Step 1 process.

Step 1:   **Write phrases or sentences in an outline format**. Pages 2 through 6 have examples of how to jot down phrases and sentences for each part of an Expository Composition.

Step 2:   **Write sentences and paragraphs in an outline format**. At this stage the phrases and sentences jotted down in Step 1 are expanded into paragraphs. Pages 7 through 12 have examples of how to do this.

Step 3:   **Write a final draft**. The student carefully edits and refines the content of Step 2, checking the grammar and mechanics, sentence patterns and word usage, and the logical structure of the writing. The student should also make sure facts are correct and that the composition meets its stated purpose. An example of a final draft is on pages 13 through 16.

How is a Topic Chosen?

Often the teacher will assign the topic. If the writer is choosing his or her own topic, it helps to make a list as follows and then choose a familiar, interesting topic from the list.

Topics for Compositions:

1. **A sport** (Examples: football, basketball, baseball, skiing, riding, swimming)
2. **A place** (Examples: beach, mountains, lake, Washington D.C., Hawaii)
3. **A person** (Examples: sports figure, movie star, grandparents, parents, police officer)
4. **An activity** (Examples: mountain climbing, going on a picnic, watching TV, dancing)
5. **An animal, vegetable, or mineral**
6. **An idea** (Examples: freedom, democracy, rights, crime)
7. **An event or phenomenon** (Examples: holiday, birthday, earthquake, tornado)
8. **An interest** (Examples: collecting stamps, horses, singing, playing the piano)

How are Sub-topics Chosen?

Sub-topics are simply different areas of the main topic. For example, if **Collecting Model Horses** is the main topic, it is easy to think up several different sub-topics about collecting model horses. Some of these sub-topics could be: **How to Start a Model Horse Collection, Different Types of Model Horses, How to Display Model Horses, Collecting Models of Specific Breeds of Horses, Accessories for Model Horses**, and so on. Each topic should have two to six sub-topics, because there will be two to six Main Body Paragraphs in the Expository Composition, and each Main Body Paragraph will discuss a different sub-topic.

WRITING STRATEGY

This book will teach you how to write an expository composition by taking you through the steps of a model composition about *dolphins*. By studying the steps of writing a composition about *dolphins*, you will understand the process you will be asked to use to write your own expository composition. At the end of the book there are blank forms for you to fill in as you write your own composition.

The process of developing an expository composition follows these steps:

FIRST: **Select a Main Topic.** Page vii has suggestions for choosing an interesting, familiar topic for the composition.

     Example of a Main Topic: Collecting Model Horses

SECOND: **Choose several different Sub-Topics** taken from the Main Topic.

     Examples of Sub-Topics:
     Sub-Topic 1: How to Start A Collection
     Sub-Topic 2: Different Types of Model Horses
     Sub-Topic 3: Collecting Models of a Specific Breed
     Sub-Topic 4: Displaying Model Horses
     Sub-Topic 5: Accessories for Model Horses

THIRD: **List each Sub-Topic on a separate page**. More than one page may be needed for each Sub-Topic. Number each Sub-Topic sheet (Sub-Topic Sheet #1, Sub-Topic Sheet #2, Sub-Topic Sheet #3, and so on). Each of these Sub-Topic Sheets will be developed into a Main Body Paragraph in Step 1 (see "FIFTH" below and the Step 1 models of Main Body Paragraphs on pages 3 through 5).

FOURTH: **Write everything you know about each Sub-Topic** on its appropriate page. Don't worry about proper writing, just jot down ideas and information.

FIFTH: **Move to Step 1.** In Step 1 you will adapt and expand the ideas and information you generated about each Sub-Topic. To understand how you will do this, study the Step 1 models for a composition about Dolphins on pages 2 through 6. Blank Step 1 forms for you to use start on page 19.

SIXTH: **Move to Step 2.** In Step 2 you will change the phrases and sentences on the Step 1 forms into complete sentences and paragraphs. To understand how you will do this, study the difference between the Step 1 models on pages 1 through 6 and the Step 2 models on pages 7 through 12. Blank Step 2 forms for you to use start on page 29.

SEVENTH: **Write your finished composition on the Final Draft forms.** Before writing your Final Draft, you will have polished your work, added transitional phrases and sentences, and perhaps even added extra paragraphs about one of the Sub-Topics. Study the Final Draft of the composition about Dolphins on pages 13 through 16 to understand how a Final Draft is written. Blank Final Draft forms for you to use start on page 39.

EXPOSITORY COMPOSITION

MODELS FOR STEP 1 OF THE WRITING PROCESS

Pages 2 through 6 contain models for Step 1 of the writing process.

The writer has already chosen a Topic: **The Dolphin**.

After brainstorming many possible Sub-topics, the writer chose three: **Impressions of dolphins from the entertainment field, Observing dolphins in their natural environment**, and **How dolphins seek food and defend against enemies**. Each Sub-topic was listed on a separate Sub-Topic Sheet. **Impressions of dolphins from the entertainment field** was on Sub-Topic Sheet #1. **Observing dolphins in their natural environment** was on Sub-Topic Sheet #2. **How dolphins seek food and defend against enemies** was on Sub-Topic Sheet #3. On each sheet the author wrote down as many supporting facts and details as possible under each Sub-Topic.

The writer also chose a purpose for the composition: **To help others learn more about dolphins in the entertainment field, in their natural environment, in their battles with enemies, in the way they care for their own, and in the way they capture food.**

Then the writer was ready to move to Step 1 of the writing process.

WRITE PHRASES/SENTENCES IN AN OUTLINE FORMAT

At this stage, the writer is jotting down words, phrases, or sentences without trying to make complete sentences or polish the writing.

Title: _____ *The Dolphin* _____

Be specific in Fact(s)/Detail(s)

I. Introductory Paragraph - tells about

   A. Composition Topic: *Dolphins are an intriguing life form.* _____

       _____

       _____

       _____

       _____

       _____

   B. Supporting Fact(s)/Detail(s): *almost human-like in playfulness and making chattering*

       sounds _____

       _____

       _____

       _____

       _____

   C. Purpose of Composition (Leads into the Main Body Paragraphs):
      1. Tells why the composition is being written
      2. Tells what the sub-topics are about in the Main Body Paragraphs

      To help others to learn more about dolphins in the entertainment field, in their

      natural environment, and in their battles with enemies, and how they care for their

      own, and how they capture food _____

      _____

STEP 1
WRITE PHRASES/SENTENCES IN AN OUTLINE FORMAT

This page develops the first sub-topic (*Impressions of dolphins from the entertainment field*) into ideas for a main body paragraph. The writer transferred ideas and information from Sub-Topic Sheet #1 onto this form without trying to make complete sentences or polish the writing.

Be specific in Fact(s)/Detail(s).

II. **Main Body Paragraph #1** - tells about...

A. Composition Sub-Topic #1: *Many of the impressions of dolphins are based on movies, television or aquariums.*

B. Supporting Fact(s)/Detail(s): *These are controlled or manipulated situations.*

C. Supporting Fact(s)/Detail(s): *Dolphin acts are primarily for entertainment and not for education.*

D. Supporting Fact(s)/Detail(s): *Financial success is the first goal of the entertainment business.*

E. Supporting Fact(s)/Detail(s): *Exploring species in their natural environment can be costly.*

F. Summarizing Statement: **First Choice** (draws logical conclusion) **or Second Choice** (restates sentence A in different words)

Information about dolphins gained from movies or aquariums is incomplete.

3

STEP 1
WRITE PHRASES/SENTENCES IN AN OUTLINE FORMAT

This page develops the second sub-topic (*Observing dolphins in their natural environment*) into ideas for a main body paragraph. The writer transferred ideas and information from Sub-Topic Sheet #2 onto this form without trying to make complete sentences or polish the writing.

Be specific in Fact(s)/Detail(s).

II. Main Body Paragraph #2 - tells about...

    A. Composition Sub-Topic #2: *Observations of dolphins in their natural environment provide important data about them.*

    B. Supporting Fact(s)/Detail(s): *Dolphins are mammals which live in the seas.*

    C. Supporting Fact(s)/Detail(s): *travel together and breathe through a blow hole*

    D. Supporting Fact(s)/Detail(s): *Male dolphins are eight or nine feet in length and weigh about eighty pounds. Females are smaller.*

    E. Supporting Fact(s)/Detail(s): *six inch beak and project a friendly image*

    F. Summarizing Statement: **First Choice** (draws logical conclusion) **or Second Choice** (restates sentence A in different words)

        They are well suited to changing situations.

4

STEP 1
WRITE PHRASES/SENTENCES IN AN OUTLINE FORMAT

This page develops the third sub-topic (*How dolphins seek food and defend against enemies*) into ideas for a main body paragraph. The writer transferred ideas and information from the Sub-Topic Sheet #3 sheet onto this form without trying to make complete sentences or polish the writing.

Be specific in Fact(s)/Detail(s).

II. Main Body Paragraph #3 - tells about...

    A. Composition Sub-Topic #3: *Dolphins cooperate in seeking food and in defending against enemies.*

    B. Supporting Fact(s)/Detail(s): *Their streamlined bodies allow for quickness to avoid predators and to capture food.*

    C. Supporting Fact(s)/Detail(s): *Dolphins may be valiant in battles.*

    D. Supporting Fact(s)/Detail(s): *Some dolphins bear scars from their battles.*

    E. Supporting Fact(s)/Detail(s): *reports of rescues by dolphins and assisting humans*

    F. Summarizing Statement: **First Choice** (draws logical conclusion) **or Second Choice** (restates sentence A in different words)

       They are set apart from most life forms by their behavior and their appearance.

STEP 1
WRITE PHRASES/SENTENCES IN AN OUTLINE FORMAT

This page develops the closing paragraph of the composition. Again, the writer is not necessarily trying to make complete sentences or polish the writing.

III.   **Closing** - tells about...

A. Restates the purpose of the composition using different words: *Learning about* *the behavior of dolphins in captivity and in their natural environment, about their* *battles with enemies and their search for food, and about helping both companions* *and humans in trouble explains why people find them intriguing.*

B. Introduces a New Idea suggested or implied by the composition: *Available data* *about dolphins is motivation for more studies.*

C. States a Significant Conclusion based on information presented in the composition: *Dolphins add to the wonder of our creation.*

EXPOSITORY COMPOSITION

MODELS FOR STEP 2 OF THE WRITING PROCESS

Pages 8 through 12 contain models for Step 2 of the writing process.

The writer has already filled out the Step 1 forms. In Step 2 the phrases and sentences on the Step 1 forms are expanded into complete sentences and paragraphs.

STEP 2
WRITE SENTENCES/PARAGRAPHS IN AN OUTLINE FORMAT

At this stage, the writer expands on the sentences and phrases from the Introductory Paragraph outline in Step 1 (see page 2) and begins polishing the writing.

Title: _The Dolphin_

Be specific in Fact(s)/Detail(s)

I. Introductory Paragraph - tells about

    A. Composition Topic: _One of the most intriguing life forms in the world is the dolphin._

        _____

        _____

        _____

        _____

        _____

    B. Supporting Fact(s)/Detail(s): _At times, the dolphin seems almost human because of his playful nature and his high-pitched chattering sounds._

        _____

        _____

        _____

    C. Purpose of Composition (Leads into the Main Body Paragraphs):
        1. Tells why the composition is being written
        2. Tells what the sub-topics are about in the Main Body Paragraphs

        These human-like qualities fuel our interest to learn more about these unusual animals, including their use in the entertainment field, their life in their natural environment, and their battles with enemies, and their search for food, and their care for their own.

8

STEP 2
WRITE SENTENCES/PARAGRAPHS IN AN OUTLINE FORMAT

The writer expands on the phrases and sentences from the Main Body Paragraph #1 outline in Step 1 (see page 3), perhaps even adding more supporting sentences. Sometimes a Sub-Topic becomes more than one paragraph when extra supporting sentences are added.

Be specific in Fact(s)/Detail(s).

II. Main Body Paragraph #1 - tells about...

A. Composition Sub-Topic #1: *Many of the impressions we have about dolphins are based on seeing them perform in movies, or on television, or at an ocean aquarium.*

B. Supporting Fact(s)/Detail(s): *Basically, these are controlled or manipulated situations in which the dolphins perform.*

C. Supporting Fact(s)/Detail(s): *Moreover, such acts are generally done for the express purpose of entertaining audiences rather than informing or educating them.*

D. Supporting Fact(s)/Detail(s): *Usually, the primary concern of the entertainment business is that its productions are a financial success.*

E. Supporting Fact(s)/Detail(s): *Time and costs, of course, make it very impractical for any enterprise to fully explore the true nature and capabilities of a specie.*

F. Summarizing Statement: **First Choice** (draws logical conclusion) **or Second Choice** (restates sentence A in different words) *Consequently, information about the dolphin gained from viewing a movie or visiting an aquarium will hardly be complete.*

9

STEP 2
WRITE SENTENCES/PARAGRAPHS IN AN OUTLINE FORMAT

The writer expands on the phrases and sentences from the Main Body Paragraph #2 outline in Step 1 (see page 4), perhaps even adding more supporting sentences. Sometimes a Sub-Topic becomes more than one paragraph when extra supporting sentences are added.

Be specific in Fact(s)/Detail(s).

II. **Main Body Paragraph #2** - tells about...

A. Composition Sub-Topic #2: *However, there is considerable data about the life and habits of the dolphin. This data is based on observations of them in their natural environment over a period of several decades.*

B. Supporting Fact(s)/Detail(s): *For instance, several species of dolphins live in seas around the world and although they are not fish, but mammals, they are excellent swimmers with the ability to react quickly and make deep dives.*

C. Supporting Fact(s)/Detail(s): *While, like fish, they may travel in "schools," they breathe through a hole in the top of their head called a blow hole.*

D. Supporting Fact(s)/Detail(s): *The adult male dolphins generally reach a length of eight or nine feet and weigh about eighty pounds: females are usually smaller than the males.*

E. Supporting Fact(s)/Detail(s): *Both the male and female have a beak about six inches long which creates the appearance of a smile and enhances their friendly image.*

F. Summarizing Statement: **First Choice** (draws logical conclusion) **or Second Choice** (restates sentence A in different words) *Thus, this combination of characteristics point to an animal that is well suited to changing situations.*

STEP 2
WRITE SENTENCES/PARAGRAPHS IN AN OUTLINE FORMAT

The writer expands on the phrases and sentences from the Main Body Paragraph #3 outline in Step 1 (see page 5), perhaps even adding more supporting sentences. Sometimes a Sub-Topic becomes more than one paragraph when extra supporting sentences are added.

Be specific in Fact(s)/Detail(s).

II. Main Body Paragraph #3 - tells about...

   A. Composition Sub-Topic #3: *While dolphins are not the largest forms of sea life, their quickness and cooperation with other dolphins are important factors in fending off sharks or killer whales as well as a means for capturing their food.*

   B. Supporting Fact(s)/Detail(s): *In other words, although an adult dolphin is significantly smaller than a whale or large shark, the dolphin's streamlined body allows him to move quickly through the water either to avoid a predator or to feed on a school of fish driven to shore by a herd of dolphins.*

   C. Supporting Fact(s)/Detail(s): *Yet, when confronted by an enemy, a dolphin may put up a valiant fight when forced to do so.*

   D. Supporting Fact(s)/Detail(s): *(Many of them bear scars which attest to their courage.)*

   E. Supporting Fact(s)/Detail(s): *In fact, there are reports of dolphins not only coming to the rescue of injured companions, but also assisting humans who are in trouble.*

   F. Summarizing Statement: **First Choice** (draws logical conclusion) **or Second Choice** (restates sentence A in different words) *Whether the actions of dolphins involved in trapping food or making dramatic rescues is due to instinct or intelligence, their behavior clearly sets them apart from most forms of life, land or sea!*

STEP 2
WRITE SENTENCES/PARAGRAPHS IN AN OUTLINE FORMAT

This page develops the closing paragraph of the composition. The writer expands on the phrases and sentences from the Closing Paragraph outline in Step 1 (see page 6), perhaps even adding more sentences. Sometimes the Closing becomes more than one paragraph when extra sentences are added.

III.   **Closing** - tells about...

A. Restates the purpose of the composition using different words:

Thus, from this brief discussion about the behavior of dolphins in captivity and in their natural environment, about their struggles with enemies and their search for food, and about assisting injured dolphins and humans in trouble, one understands why many people find them so intriguing.

B. Introduces a New Idea suggested or implied by the composition:

Furthermore, the fascinating data already gathered about dolphins is motivation for continued studies of them.

C. States a Significant Conclusion based on information presented in the composition:

Finally, even armed with less than full knowledge of the dolphin, one can still not help being struck by the wonder and mystery of our creation.

EXPOSITORY COMPOSITION

STEP 3

MODEL FINAL DRAFT

As you will see in this model of a final draft based on the model Step 1 and Step 2 outline sheets, the writer has polished the work, added transitional phrases and sentences, and even added an extra paragraph about one of the Sub-Topics.

As you read the Final Draft of the expository composition about Dolphins, compare it to the Step 2 sheets on pages 8 through 12. Notice how the author expanded his original Main Paragraph #3 to two paragraphs. Also, notice the use of transition sentences, phrases, and words.

STEP 3
MODEL FINAL DRAFT

Student's Name _____

Course_____

Date_____

The Dolphin

<table>
<tr>
<td>Introductory Paragraph</td>
<td>One of the most intriguing life forms in the world is the dolphin. At times, the dolphin seems almost human because of his playful nature and his high-pitched chattering sounds. These human-like qualities fuel our interest to learn more about these unusual animals, including their use in the field of entertainment, their natural environments, and their battles with enemies, and their search for food and their care for their own.</td>
</tr>
<tr>
<td>Main Body Paragraph #1</td>
<td>Many of the impressions which we have about dolphins are based on seeing them perform in movies or on television, or seeing them at an ocean aquarium. Basically, these are controlled or manipulated situations in which the dolphins perform. Moreover, such acts are done primarily for the express purpose of entertaining audiences rather than educating or informing them. Generally, the main concern of the entertainment business is that its productions are a financial success. Time and cost, of course, make it very impractical for an enterprise to fully explore the true nature and capabilities of a specie. Consequently, information about the dolphin gained from viewing a movie, or even visiting an aquarium, will hardly be complete.</td>
</tr>
<tr>
<td>Main Body Paragraph #2</td>
<td>However, there is a considerable amount of data about the life and habits of dolphins based on observations of them in their natural environment over a period of decades. For instance, several species of dolphins live in seas around the world, and although they are not</td>
</tr>
</table>

14

Student's Name _____

fish, but mammals, they are excellent swimmers with the ability to react quickly and make deep dives. While, like fish, they may travel in "schools," they breathe through a hole in the top of their heads called a blow hole. The adult male dolphins, as a rule, reach a length of eight or nine feet and weigh about eighty pounds: females are usually smaller than the males. Both the male and female have a beak about six inches long that creates the appearance of a smile and enhances their friendly image. Thus, this combination of characteristics points to an animal which is well suited to changing conditions.

Although dolphins are not the largest forms of sea life, their agility and cooperative behavior are important factors in trying to fend off sharks or killer whales as well as key elements in their ability to capture food. In other words, while an adult dolphin is significantly smaller than a whale or a large shark, the dolphin's streamlined body allows him to move quickly through the water either to avoid a predator or to feed on a school of fish.

Main Body Paragraph #3

Yet, when confronted by an enemy, a dolphin may put up a valiant defense when forced to do so. (Many of them bear scars which attest to their courage.) In fact, there are reports of dolphins not only coming to the rescue of injured companions, but also assisting humans who are in trouble. Whether the actions of dolphins involved in trapping food or making dramatic rescues is due to instinct or intelligence, their behavior clearly sets them apart from most forms of life, land or sea.

Main Body Paragraph #4

STEP 3
MODEL FINAL DRAFT

Student's Name _____

Closing Paragraph

> *Thus, from this brief discussion about the behavior of dolphins in captivity and in their natural environment, about their struggles with enemies and their search for food, and about their assisting injured companions and humans in trouble, one can easily understand why many people find them so intriguing. Moreover, the fascinating data already accumulated about dolphins is sufficient motivation for continuing the study of them. Finally, although armed with less than full knowledge of the dolphin's life and behavior patterns, one still cannot help being struck by the wonders and mysteries found in our creation.*

STUDENT WRITING STRATEGY

This section contains forms for you to fill in for Step 1, Step 2, and the Final Draft of writing your own expository composition. This is the process you will use in writing.

FIRST: **Select a Main Topic.** Page vii has suggestions for choosing an interesting, familiar topic for the composition.

         Example of a Main Topic: Collecting Model Horses

SECOND: **Choose several different Sub-Topics** taken from the Main Topic.

         Examples of Sub-Topics:
         Sub-Topic 1: How to Start A Collection
         Sub-Topic 2: Different Types of Model Horses
         Sub-Topic 3: Collecting Models of a Specific Breed
         Sub-Topic 4: Displaying Model Horses
         Sub-Topic 5: Accessories for Model Horses

THIRD: **Pick two to six Sub-Topics and list each Sub-Topic on a separate page.** Number each Sub-Topic sheet (Sub-Topic Sheet # 1, Sub-Topic Sheet #2, and so on). Each of these Sub-Topic sheets will be developed into a Main Body Paragraph in Step 1 (see "FIFTH" below and the Step 1 models of Main Body Paragraphs on pages 3 through 6). More than one page may be needed for each Sub-Topic.

FOURTH: **Write everything you know about each Sub-Topic** on its appropriate page. Don't worry about proper writing, just jot down ideas and information.

FIFTH: **Move to the Step 1 forms starting on page 19.** In Step 1 you will adapt and expand the ideas and information you generated about each Sub-Topic. To understand how you will do this, study the Step 1 models for a composition about Dolphins on pages 2 through 6.

SIXTH: **Move to the Step 2 forms starting on page 29.** In Step 2 you will change the phrases and sentences on the Step 1 forms into complete sentences and paragraphs. To understand how you will do this, study the difference between the Step 1 models on pages 2 through 6 and the Step 2 models on pages 8 through 12.

SEVENTH: **Write your finished composition on the Step 3 Final Draft forms on page 39.** Before writing your Final Draft, you will have polished your work, added transitional phrases and sentences, and perhaps even added extra paragraphs about one of the Sub-Topics. To understand how you will do this, study the difference between the Step 2 models on pages 8 through 12 and the Step 3 Final Draft models on pages 13 through 16.

TIPS ON DEVELOPING MAIN BODY PARAGRAPHS

Sometimes when trying to develop a composition Sub-Topic in one of the Main Body Paragraphs, you will run out of ideas for the Supporting Fact(s)/Detail(s) sentences. What can you do?

First, you should try and think of more information about the Sub-Topic.

Second, you find an action type sentence (a sentence that tells about something that happened, is happening, or will happen) you have already written about the Sub-Topic. Ask three key questions about that sentence. The answer to each question should generate a new idea which can be used to fill in an unused space for a Supporting Fact(s)/Detail(s) Sentence.

Example of an Action Type Sentence:
When white-water rafting, you should be wearing a proper life jacket at all times.

Key Question #1:
What happens if it is not done?

Answer (New Idea) generated by Key Question #1:
Failure to wear a proper life jacket when white-water rafting could result in a serious injury or even death.

This answer (New Idea) can be used as a Supporting Fact(s)/Detail(s) sentence.

Key Question #2:
What happens if it is done?

Answer (New Idea) generated by Key Question #2:
By wearing a life jacket approved for white water rafting, you may not only save yourself from injury or death, but you will also be better prepared to assist someone else who has fallen overboard.

This answer (New Idea) can be used as a Supporting Fact(s)/Detail(s) sentence.

Key Question #3:
If it is done, what preparations or skills are needed?

Answer (New Idea) generated by Key Question #3:
Before white-water rafting, you should visit a sporting goods store and purchase a life jacket specifically designed to keep you afloat if you should fall into the rapids.

This answer (New Idea) can be used as a Supporting Fact(s)/Detail(s) sentence.

STEP 1

WRITING FORMS

FOR PHRASES/SENTENCES

STEP 1
WRITE PHRASES/SENTENCES IN AN OUTLINE FORMAT

Title: _____

Be specific in Fact(s)/Detail(s)

I. Introductory Paragraph - tells about

   A. Composition Topic: _____

     _____

     _____

     _____

     _____

     _____

   B. Supporting Fact(s)/Detail(s): _____

     _____

     _____

     _____

     _____

   C. Purpose of Composition (Leads into the Main Body Paragraphs):
     1. Tells why the composition is being written
     2. Tells what the sub-topics are about in the Main Body Paragraphs

     _____

     _____

     _____

     _____

STEP 1
WRITE PHRASES/SENTENCES IN AN OUTLINE FORMAT

This page develops your first sub-topic into ideas for a main body paragraph. Transfer ideas and information from the Sub-Topic Sheet #1 onto this form without trying to make complete sentences or polish the writing. (See page 18 for Tips on Developing Main Body Paragraphs.)

Be specific in Fact(s)/Detail(s).

II. Main Body Paragraph #1 - tells about...

    A. Composition Sub-Topic #1: _____

    _____

    _____

    B. Supporting Fact(s)/Detail(s): _____

    _____

    _____

    C. Supporting Fact(s)/Detail(s): _____

    _____

    _____

    D. Supporting Fact(s)/Detail(s): _____

    _____

    _____

    E. Supporting Fact(s)/Detail(s): _____

    _____

    _____

    F. Summarizing Statement: **First Choice** (draws logical conclusion) **or Second Choice** (restates sentence A in different words) _____

    _____

    _____

    _____

STEP 1
WRITE PHRASES/SENTENCES IN AN OUTLINE FORMAT

This page develops your second sub-topic into ideas for a main body paragraph. Transfer ideas and information from the Sub-Topic Sheet #2 onto this form without trying to make complete sentences or polish the writing. (See page 18 for Tips on Developing Main Body Paragraphs.)

Be specific in Fact(s)/Detail(s).

II. Main Body Paragraph #2 - tells about...

A. Composition Sub-Topic #2: _____

_____

_____

B. Supporting Fact(s)/Detail(s): _____

_____

_____

C. Supporting Fact(s)/Detail(s): _____

_____

_____

D. Supporting Fact(s)/Detail(s): _____

_____

_____

E. Supporting Fact(s)/Detail(s): _____

_____

_____

F. Summarizing Statement: **First Choice** (draws logical conclusion) **or Second Choice** (restates sentence A in different words) _____

_____

_____

_____

22

STEP 1
WRITE PHRASES/SENTENCES IN AN OUTLINE FORMAT

This page develops your third sub-topic into ideas for a main body paragraph. Transfer ideas and information from the Sub-Topic Sheet #3 onto this form without trying to make complete sentences or polish the writing. (See page 18 for Tips on Developing Main Body Paragraphs.)

Be specific in Fact(s)/Detail(s).

II. Main Body Paragraph #3 - tells about...

A. Composition Sub-Topic #3: _____

_____

_____

B. Supporting Fact(s)/Detail(s): _____

_____

_____

C. Supporting Fact(s)/Detail(s): _____

_____

_____

D. Supporting Fact(s)/Detail(s): _____

_____

_____

E. Supporting Fact(s)/Detail(s): _____

_____

_____

F. Summarizing Statement: **First Choice** (draws logical conclusion) **or Second Choice** (restates sentence A in different words) _____

_____

_____

_____

STEP 1
WRITE PHRASES/SENTENCES IN AN OUTLINE FORMAT

This page develops your fourth sub-topic into ideas for a main body paragraph. Transfer ideas and information from Sub-Topic Sheet #4 onto this form without trying to make complete sentences or polish the writing. (See page 18 for Tips on Developing Main Body Paragraphs.)

Be specific in Fact(s)/Detail(s).

II. Main Body Paragraph #4 - tells about...

    A. Composition Sub-Topic #4: _____

_____

_____

    B. Supporting Fact(s)/Detail(s): _____

_____

_____

    C. Supporting Fact(s)/Detail(s): _____

_____

_____

    D. Supporting Fact(s)/Detail(s): _____

_____

_____

    E. Supporting Fact(s)/Detail(s): _____

_____

_____

    F. Summarizing Statement: **First Choice** (draws logical conclusion) **or Second Choice** (restates sentence A in different words) _____

_____

_____

_____

STEP 1
WRITE PHRASES/SENTENCES IN AN OUTLINE FORMAT

This page develops your fifth sub-topic into ideas for a main body paragraph. Transfer ideas and information from the Sub-Topic Sheet #5 onto this form without trying to make complete sentences or polish the writing. (See page 18 for Tips on Developing Main Body Paragraphs.)

Be specific in Fact(s)/Detail(s).

II. Main Body Paragraph #5 - tells about...

    A. Composition Sub-Topic #5: _____

    _____

    _____

    B. Supporting Fact(s)/Detail(s): _____

    _____

    _____

    C. Supporting Fact(s)/Detail(s): _____

    _____

    _____

    D. Supporting Fact(s)/Detail(s): _____

    _____

    _____

    E. Supporting Fact(s)/Detail(s): _____

    _____

    _____

    F. Summarizing Statement: **First Choice** (draws logical conclusion) **or Second Choice** (restates sentence A in different words) _____

    _____

    _____

    _____

25

STEP 1
WRITE PHRASES/SENTENCES IN AN OUTLINE FORMAT

This page develops your sixth sub-topic into ideas for a main body paragraph. Transfer ideas and information from Sub-Topic Sheet #6 onto this form without trying to make complete sentences or polish the writing. (See page 18 for Tips on Developing Main Body Paragraphs.)

Be specific in Fact(s)/Detail(s).

II. Main Body Paragraph #6 - tells about...

    A. Composition Sub-Topic #6: _____

    _____

    _____

    B. Supporting Fact(s)/Detail(s): _____

    _____

    _____

    C. Supporting Fact(s)/Detail(s): _____

    _____

    _____

    D. Supporting Fact(s)/Detail(s): _____

    _____

    _____

    E. Supporting Fact(s)/Detail(s): _____

    _____

    _____

    F. Summarizing Statement: **First Choice** (draws logical conclusion) **or Second Choice** (restates sentence A in different words) _____

    _____

    _____

    _____

WRITE PHRASES/SENTENCES IN AN OUTLINE FORMAT

This page develops the closing paragraph of the composition. Again, you are not necessarily trying to make complete sentences or polish the writing.

III. **Closing** - tells about...

    A. Restates the purpose of the composition using different words: _____

       _____

       _____

       _____

       _____

       _____

    B. Introduces a New Idea suggested or implied by the composition: _____

       _____

       _____

       _____

       _____

    C. States a Significant Conclusion based on information presented in the composition:

       _____

       _____

       _____

       _____

       _____

STEP 2

WRITING FORMS

FOR SENTENCES/PARAGRAPHS

WRITE SENTENCES/PARAGRAPHS IN AN OUTLINE FORMAT

At this stage, you will expand on the sentences and phrases from the Introductory Paragraph outline in Step 1 (page 20) and begin polishing the writing.

Title: _How Sun worship became Christmas_

Be specific in Fact(s)/Detail(s)

I. Introductory Paragraph - tells about

   A. Composition Topic: _The origins of Christmas_

         _____

         _____

         _____

         _____

   B. Supporting Fact(s)/Detail(s): _Christmas derived from pagan_
festivals.

   C. Purpose of Composition (Leads into the Main Body Paragraphs):
      1. Tells why the composition is being written
      2. Tells what the sub-topics are about in the Main Body Paragraphs

      To explain that Christmas is a pagan holiday.
      the origins

STEP 2
WRITE SENTENCES/PARAGRAPHS IN AN OUTLINE FORMAT

Now you will expand on the phrases and sentences from the Main Body Paragraph #1 outline in Step 1 (page 21), perhaps even adding more supporting sentences. Sometimes a Sub-Topic becomes more than one paragraph when extra supporting sentences are added.

Be specific in Fact(s)/Detail(s).

II. Main Body Paragraph #1 - tells about...

A. Composition Sub-Topic #1: It started off with the whole world worshiping Mithra, the Persian god of light, the sun

B. Supporting Fact(s)/Detail(s): On December 25, the Romans glorified + worshiped the ancient Persian god of light, Mithra.

C. Supporting Fact(s)/Detail(s): The Egyptians worshiped Raa. Raa was said to have sent out rays in forms of flowers. He also had his own town called Heliopolis.

D. Supporting Fact(s)/Detail(s): Greeks called the sun Helios.

E. Supporting Fact(s)/Detail(s):

F. Summarizing Statement: **First Choice** (draws logical conclusion) **or Second Choice** (restates sentence A in different words) How did sun worship become Son worship? Now that we have established the fact that the whole world was worshiping the sun, what how does this tie in with Christmas?

31

STEP 2
WRITE SENTENCES/PARAGRAPHS IN AN OUTLINE FORMAT

On this page you will expand on the phrases and sentences from the Main Body Paragraph #2 outline in Step 1 (page 22), perhaps even adding more supporting sentences. Sometimes a Sub-Topic becomes more than one paragraph when extra supporting sentences are added.

Be specific in Fact(s)/Detail(s).

II. Main Body Paragraph #2 - tells about...

A. Composition Sub-Topic #2: _Christians enter the scene._

_____

_____

B. Supporting Fact(s)/Detail(s): _The Christians came marching 3 by 3 hurrah, hurrah! The only problem is that they cut too much slack for these people..._

C. Supporting Fact(s)/Detail(s): _Christians allowed them to keep their pagan festivals + traditions. The only schnit bit they changed was worshing Christ, the Son of God._

D. Supporting Fact(s)/Detail(s): _The Roman Cathic Church also made Dec. 25 the official birthday of Christ as to give meaning to Pagan traditions!_

E. Supporting Fact(s)/Detail(s): _____

_____

_____

F. Summarizing Statement: **First Choice** (draws logical conclusion) **or Second Choice** (restates sentence A in different words) _____

_____

_____

_____

STEP 2
WRITE SENTENCES/PARAGRAPHS IN AN OUTLINE FORMAT

On this page you will expand on the phrases and sentences from the Main Body Paragraph #3 outline in Step 1 (page 23), perhaps even adding more supporting sentences. Sometimes a Sub-Topic becomes more than one paragraph when extra supporting sentences are added.

Be specific in Fact(s)/Detail(s).

II. Main Body Paragraph #3 - tells about...

    A. Composition Sub-Topic #3: _____

_____

_____

    B. Supporting Fact(s)/Detail(s): _____

_____

_____

    C. Supporting Fact(s)/Detail(s): _____

_____

_____

    D. Supporting Fact(s)/Detail(s): _____

_____

_____

    E. Supporting Fact(s)/Detail(s): _____

_____

_____

    F. Summarizing Statement: **First Choice** (draws logical conclusion) **or Second Choice** (restates sentence A in different words) _____

_____

_____

_____

STEP 2
WRITE SENTENCES/PARAGRAPHS IN AN OUTLINE FORMAT

On this page you will expand on the phrases and sentences from the Main Body Paragraph #4 outline in Step 1(page 24), perhaps even adding more supporting sentences. Sometimes a Sub-Topic becomes more than one paragraph when extra supporting sentences are added.

Be specific in Fact(s)/Detail(s).

II. Main Body Paragraph #4 - tells about...

   A. Composition Sub-Topic #4: _____

   _____

   _____

   B. Supporting Fact(s)/Detail(s): _____

   _____

   _____

   C. Supporting Fact(s)/Detail(s): _____

   _____

   _____

   D. Supporting Fact(s)/Detail(s): _____

   _____

   _____

   E. Supporting Fact(s)/Detail(s): _____

   _____

   _____

   F. Summarizing Statement: **First Choice** (draws logical conclusion) **or Second Choice** (restates sentence A in different words) _____

   _____

   _____

   _____

WRITE SENTENCES/PARAGRAPHS IN AN OUTLINE FORMAT

On this page you will expand on the phrases and sentences from the Main Body Paragraph #5 outline in Step 1 (page 25), perhaps even adding more supporting sentences. Sometimes a Sub-Topic becomes more than one paragraph when extra supporting sentences are added.

Be specific in Fact(s)/Detail(s).

II. Main Body Paragraph #5 - tells about...

    A. Composition Sub-Topic #5: _____

       _____

       _____

    B. Supporting Fact(s)/Detail(s): _____

       _____

       _____

    C. Supporting Fact(s)/Detail(s): _____

       _____

       _____

    D. Supporting Fact(s)/Detail(s): _____

       _____

       _____

    E. Supporting Fact(s)/Detail(s): _____

       _____

       _____

    F. Summarizing Statement: **First Choice** (draws logical conclusion) **or Second Choice** (restates sentence A in different words) _____

       _____

       _____

       _____

STEP 2
WRITE SENTENCES/PARAGRAPHS IN AN OUTLINE FORMAT

On this page you will expand on the phrases and sentences from the Main Body Paragraph #6 outline in Step 1 (page 26), perhaps even adding more supporting sentences. Sometimes a Sub-Topic becomes more than one paragraph when extra supporting sentences are added.

Be specific in Fact(s)/Detail(s).

II. Main Body Paragraph #6 - tells about...

A. Composition Sub-Topic #6: _____

_____

_____

B. Supporting Fact(s)/Detail(s): _____

_____

_____

C. Supporting Fact(s)/Detail(s): _____

_____

_____

D. Supporting Fact(s)/Detail(s): _____

_____

_____

E. Supporting Fact(s)/Detail(s): _____

_____

_____

F. Summarizing Statement: **First Choice** (draws logical conclusion) **or Second Choice** (restates sentence A in different words) _____

_____

_____

_____

STEP 2
WRITE SENTENCES/PARAGRAPHS IN AN OUTLINE FORMAT

This page develops the closing paragraph of the composition. You will expand on the phrases and sentences from the Closing Paragraph outline in Step 1 (page 27), perhaps even adding more sentences. Sometimes the Closing becomes more than one paragraph when extra sentences are added.

III.   **Closing** - tells about...

    A. Restates the purpose of the composition using different words: _____

        _____

        _____

        _____

        _____

    B. Introduces a New Idea suggested or implied by the composition: _____

        _____

        _____

        _____

    C. States a Significant Conclusion based on information presented in the composition:

        _____

        _____

        _____

        _____

        _____

WRITING THE FINAL DRAFT

The next step to writing an expository composition is Step 3: the Final Draft. After the Step 2 outlines have been filled in and before writing the Final Draft, you should carefully edit the content of each Step 2 page. Some of the types of editing you will need to do are:

- make sure that your grammar, punctuation, and spelling are correct
- check that you have varied your words (haven't used the same words over and over)
- make sure that the facts you wrote are correct
- check the writing structure to make sure it follows a logical pattern
- make sure that the composition meets its stated purpose

A key element to a logical, smooth-flowing paper is the use of transitions. You should check to see if transitions are needed between sentences, paragraphs, and pages. A simple test to determine whether a transition is needed between pages is as follows:

Read the last one or two sentences at the end of the first page and read the first sentence on the next page. If the two pages do not seem connected or linked or there is an abrupt break between them, you may need to rewrite the first sentence on the second page or add a transition word, phrase, or sentence between the first and second pages. Some of the more common transitions used in compositions are:

A. Moreover, Furthermore, In addition
B. In fact, For instance, For example
C. Specifically, In other words, In short
D. However, Yet, Still, On the other hand
E. Although, Even though, Regardless
F. Perhaps, Thus, Then, While
G. Not only....but also, Nevertheless
H. Now, Next, Meanwhile, In the meantime
I. Finally, Lastly, Consequently, Hence, Since

STEP 3

FINAL DRAFT

WRITING FORMS

STEP 3
FINAL DRAFT

Student's Name _____

Course_____

Date_____

Title: _____

STEP 3
FINAL DRAFT

Student's Name _____

STEP 3
FINAL DRAFT

Student's Name _____

STEP 3
FINAL DRAFT

Student's Name _____

STEP 3
FINAL DRAFT

Student's Name _____

STEP 3
FINAL DRAFT

Student's Name _____

STEP 3
FINAL DRAFT

Student's Name _____

Student's Name _____

STEP 3
FINAL DRAFT

Student's Name _____